Bibliographical Series
of Supplements to 'British Book News'
on Writers and Their Work

★

GENERAL EDITOR
Geoffrey Bullough

¶ ALFRED TENNYSON was born on 6 August 1809 at Somersby, Lincolnshire. He died on 6 October 1892 at Aldworth, near Haselmere, Surrey, and is buried in Westminster Abbey.

TENNYSON

from a painting by SAMUEL LAURENCE
in the National Portrait Gallery

TENNYSON

by

F. L. LUCAS

PUBLISHED FOR
THE BRITISH COUNCIL
AND THE NATIONAL BOOK LEAGUE
BY LONGMANS, GREEN & CO

LONGMANS GREEN & CO LTD
48 Grosvenor Street, London, W.1

*Associated companies, branches and
representatives throughout the world*

First published 1957
Reprinted with additions to bibliography 1961, 1966
First edition © F. L. Lucas 1957

*Printed in Great Britain
F. Mildner & Sons, London, E.C.1*

TENNYSON

I

TAINE'S *Histoire de la Littérature Anglaise* (1863-4), often erratic, yet always lively with ideas, finds its climax and its end in a contrast that is still vivid, between England and France, Tennyson and Alfred de Musset. First, Taine lands us 'at Newhaven or Dover', and leads us through the rolling greenness of the English countryside, its grey medieval towers, its comfortable manors and villas—homes of a healthy, practical, cultivated gentry, with their gracious, balanced womenfolk, their demure, white-shouldered daughters. Such was the land, such the public, of Tennyson.

Then Taine wheels back southward on Calais, and whirls us towards Paris. Here, too, there unfolds a countryside almost as green, dotted likewise, though less lavishly, with affluent country houses; yet here in France the provinces remain dominated by Paris, 'like a snail led by a butterfly'. And Paris? A glare of lights that fall garishly on jostling boulevard, grey *faubourg*, squalid alley; on pallid faces in salon or café, tense with the strain of a fevered restlessness. And yet what a vibration of ideas, what gay, unflinching, uninhibited discussion of all life's values and all life's riddles! Such is the world where Alfred de Musset once loved and agonized—far less happy, Taine admits, than 'that other poet in the Isle of Wight, among his roses and honey-suckles'. Yet no matter. Musset was not, like Tennyson, 'content to taste and enjoy; he stamped his mark on human thought . . . He tore, despairing, from his entrails the idea he had conceived, and held it up before mankind, bleeding, but alive . . . The world that listened to Tennyson is of more worth than our aristocracy of bourgeois and Bohemians: but I love Alfred de Musset better than Tennyson.'

Matthew Arnold, who was a little apt to inspect poets, as he inspected schools, for their educational value, took a somewhat similar view—Musset and Heine were 'far more profitable studies'. For Tennyson was 'deficient in intellectual power; and no modern poet can make very much of his business unless he is pre-eminently strong in this.'

Both Taine and Arnold are, in effect, suggesting that Tennyson's poetry might be called, like one of his early poems, 'Supposed Confessions of a Second-rate Sensitive Mind'. And this view is, I think, important, not because it is true, but because it is false—or rather one of those half-truths more misleading than many falsehoods. For though it is no longer the fashion to sneer at Tennyson as it sometimes was earlier in this century,[1] and though a more understanding interest in his personality has been awakened by Sir Harold Nicolson's brilliant study and Sir Charles Tennyson's impressive biography, still in modern appreciations of his work there remains often something of the timid or the tepid.[2] This may be partly because, in literary taste, ages of sugar alternate with ages of pepper, and ours is an age of pepper; but partly also, I suspect, because many moderns do not think highly of Tennyson as a thinker. For some, he doubts too much; for some, too little. Recently, when I asked a clever Indian professor if Tennyson were still much read in India, he replied that Tennyson's thought seemed out of date. But why read him for his 'thought'?—why not, like Sappho, or Catullus, or Ronsard, for his poetry? No one

[1] Compare the moving lines of Hardy in *Late Lyrics and Earlier* (1922):
> The bower we shrined to Tennyson,
>> Gentlemen,
> Is roof-wrecked; damps there drip upon
> Sagged seats, the creeper-nails are rust,
> The spider is sole denizen;
> E'en she who read those rhymes is dust,
>> Gentlemen.

('An Ancient to Ancients')

[2] From information kindly supplied by publishers, particularly Messrs. Macmillan and the Oxford Press, I get the impression that, at a rough guess, editions and selections of Tennyson still sell at the rate of something like ten thousand copies a year. (And it has to be remembered that he is also easily bought second-hand.) Many living writers would not be ill-content to do as well.

expects Pope's ideas to be up to date. In a century or so no
one will expect it of Tennyson. With either, the poetry will
be enough. Then why wait?

Besides, what after all were the superior ideas found by
Taine in Alfred de Musset? That life is a ghastly vanity of
vanities, where the one thing not vanity is to be constantly
in love. One may be bewitched by the grace of Musset's
lyrics, enchanted by the gaiety of his plays. But I should
have thought his strength lay in his youthful passion and his
wit, not his philosophy.[1] What, again, were the ideas of
Arnold himself? That life is a battlefield where ignorant
armies clash in darkness; and that there is no help for it but
a sad stoicism, loyal love, and trust in that rather dank con-
cept, a Stream of Tendency making for righteousness.
Brave, noble—but philosophy? What remains, in the end,
but a mournful, musical voice crying through the night? I
see no reason to believe that Arnold really possessed more
'intellectual power' than the Tennyson he condemned.

What Shakespeare's philosophy was is debated, and even
whether he had any. Profundities, indeed, are fathered on
him by professors. Yet for all his ideas Bernard Shaw was
not prepared to bid twopence; and George Moore wished
them all expunged. Milton thought he had justified God's
ways; but few of his readers still think so, or are much
edified, in *Samson*, by the mass-conversion of Philistines to
pulp. Pope gathered together the philosophies of his genera-
tion: but there are no Warburtons to defend his dogmas now.
For thorough Wordsworthians, no doubt, Wordsworthian-
ism is a religion; yet many others love his poetry of mountain and cottage without caring a pin for what they regard
as his mystical moonshine. Byron, so even Arnold admitted,

---

[1] Compare the harsh strictures passed on him by Baudelaire—'*impuis-
sance totale à comprendre le travail*', '*poésie d'échelles de soie*'; and Louis
Bouilhet:

> *Je déteste surtout le barde à l'œil humide*
> *Qui regarde une étoile en murmurant un nom,*
> *Et pour qui la nature immense serait vide*
> *S'il ne portait en croupe ou Lisette ou Ninon.*

'taught us nothing': but his passion and his personality remain. Browning was once among the prophets; but where now are the Browning Societies? Yet his lyrics endure. Christina Rossetti was all her life as naïve as a novice in a medieval nunnery. '*Quant à Victor Hugo*', writes Anatole France, '*il naquit et mourut enfant de chœur. En toutes choses il changeait d'idées à mesure que les idées changeaient autour de lui.*' After all, the Muse did not say to Sidney: 'Look in thy *head*, and write'.

If Tennyson, then, seems an unsuccessful philosopher, the same has been true of most poets (and, the poets might add, of most philosophers). 'The Art of Discourse,' wrote Ibn Khaldun (1332–1406), 'whether in verse or prose, lies only in words, not in ideas . . . just as the vessels wherein water is drawn from the sea may be of gold, or silver, or pottery, or glass, or earthenware.' Tennyson was a goldsmith.

What is the real place of ideas in poetry? In ancient Greece, when verse was young and prose still a lisping infant, poets were honoured as teachers, and thinkers wrote in metre. But soon the philosophers became prose specialists, and despised the poets as dreaming amateurs. Yet a poet, like any other human adult, must have a view of life or remain a mental earthworm; secondly, his view of life can add unity to his work (as with Ibsen or Hardy); thirdly, belief in the importance of his ideas can save a poet from the demoralizing sense of being merely 'the idle singer of an empty day'; fourthly, even if a poet's ideas are nothing new, he may be able to make his hearers feel intensely, not simply see, how true they are; and, fifthly, when a reader does share the poet's beliefs (as a Roman Catholic with Francis Thompson, or a sceptic with Thomas Hardy), his sympathy with the poetry may become vastly deepeneed and heightened.

For these reasons, ideas seem to me important in poetry; yet far from all-important. Tennyson's ideas mattered deeply to him; deeply to his age; but much less to most of us—indeed they often become obstacles to surmount or avoid. By nature he was passionately absorbed in the riddles of the painful earth; as he grew prominent, the prophet's mantle was thrust upon him;[1] and at times, one may feel, his song grew smothered by it. Today bookstalls no longer display *Sermonettes from Tennyson*. And if I have begun by talking so much of Tennyson's ideas, it is because they have been ceaselessly talked of, and it seems to me time we talked less of them. In actual intelligence Tennyson was, I imagine, well above most of his readers and many of his critics; it seems a little exacting to demand so much more. He was acute enough to dread that the coming world would darken,[2] and its skies be filled with brutalized war; to hope for something like the British Commonwealth, and something like the United Nations. But successful prophecies soon lose all but historic interest: it is the poetry that matters. Wise readers do not go to Virgil for *sortes Virgilianae*.

Yet there is another gift far more important, I think, to a poet than philosophy—personality. Without personality, it is hard to have a style; without style, it is hard to last. And personality Tennyson most certainly had. Indeed he had two. Seen with sympathy (and what is criticism without?) he becomes a moving character, in his affection, generosity, and simplicity. But the poet of 'The Two Voices' was himself double, like a double star with a dimmer body obscuring at intervals the splendour of the other that it circles round. This could be perceived from his works alone; but to see it fully there is need of biography as well. Not that his life was dramatic, like Byron's, or Hugo's, or Tolstoy's (better for him, perhaps, had it been more so). It is not what he did that

---

[1] For example, to quote one instance among many, he was thus adjured to stand up and be a Moses by *Hogg's Weekly Instructor* (25-12-1847): 'Why does not Alfred Tennyson leave the Midian of his retirement to point the people's way to the coming Canaan?' What a period! There were no Hoggs by the Ilissus (though there was, indeed, a Plato).

[2] e.g. in 1886: 'You must not be surprised at anything that comes to pass in the next fifty years. All ages are ages of transition, but this is an awful moment of transition.'

matters, but what he was. Therefore the bare facts of his career are best confined, I think, to the bare light of a chronological table.

1809 6 August. Born at Somersby, Lincolnshire, third surviving son of the Rector, Dr George Tennyson.

1811 Birth of his future friend, Arthur Hallam.

1816–20 Unhappy at Louth Grammar School.

c. 1823–4 'The Devil and the Lady' written (one of the most astonishing works ever composed by a boy of fourteen).

1827 *Poems by Two Brothers* (with Charles Tennyson; including three or four pieces by Frederick).

1828–31 Trinity College, Cambridge.

1830 *Poems, Chiefly Lyrical.* Journey with Hallam to the Pyrenees, carrying funds for Spanish insurgents against King Ferdinand.

1831 (February). Hallam engaged to Tennyson's sister, Emily. (March). Tennyson's father dies.

1832 (May). The 1830 *Poems* reviewed, with mingled jeers and praises, by Christopher North in *Blackwood's.* (December). *Poems.* (Dated 1833.)

1833 (April). Savage review by J. M. Croker in *The Quarterly* (15 September). Sudden death of Hallam in Vienna.

1836 The poet's brother, Charles Tennyson Turner, marries Louisa Sellwood; with her elder sister Emily, the future Lady Tennyson, as bridesmaid.

1838 Engagement to Emily Sellwood.

1840 Engagement broken off, for financial and other reasons.

1842 *Poems.* (Eleven editions by 1856.)

1843 Loses his capital (£3,000) in Dr Allen's scheme for wood-carving by machinery. (Part was later recovered on Allen's death.)

1844 Praised by Poe as perhaps 'the greatest of poets'.

1845 Praised by Wordsworth as 'the first of our living poets' Pension of £200 granted by Peel.

1847 *The Princess.* (Nine editions by 1860).

1850 *In Memoriam.* (Three editions, the first anonymous; seven by 1856.)
(June). Marriage to Emily Sellwood.
(November). Poet Laureate.

1852 *Ode on the death of the Duke of Wellington.*
1853 Settles at Farringford, Isle of Wight.
1854 'Charge of the Light Brigade'. (2,000 copies pinted for
      the troops in the Crimea.)
1855 *Maud and Other Poems.* (Nine editions by 1862.)
1859 *Idylls of the King.* ('Enid', 'Vivien', 'Elaine',' Guinevere'.
      Over 10,000 sold in the first week. Eleven editions by
      1870.)
1864 *Enoch Arden.* (Quickly sold 60,000 copies.)
1868 Building of Aldworth (Surrey) begun.
1869 *The Holy Grail and Other Poems.*
1872 *Gareth and Lynette.*
1875 *Queen Mary.*
1877 *Harold.*
1879 *Becket.*
1880 *Ballads and Other Poems.*
1883 Peerage accepted.
1885 *Tiresias, and Other Poems.*
1889 *Demeter, and Other Poems.*
1892 6 October. Death at Aldworth; burial in Westminster
      Abbey.[1] *The Death of Oenone and Other Peoms.*

II

So outlined, it looks an amazingly prosperous career. In
particular, its last forty-two years are a long series of triumphs
—Laureateship, peerage, Farringford, Aldworth, Westminster Abbey. No English poet has ever been so rewarded.
No wonder Taine could picture Tennyson embowered in
honeysuckle and roses. Yet the first forty-one years had
often been darkened; and to the end of that long life there
lurked always in the background the haunting shadow of
melancholia—of 'immeasurable sadness'.

Tennyson had come into the world with a silver tongue
in his mouth, but by no means with a silver spoon. His

[1] Better, I feel, if this poet of nature had been laid, not among the sooty
stones of London, but rather, like some old chieftain, beneath the cross on
High Down above The Needles, looking along the white cliffs of the
Channel to the green barrows of prehistory upon Brightstone Down.

grandfather, indeed, was rich—a hard-headed solicitor and landowner in Lincolnshire; of Yorkshire yeoman stock on the paternal side, but claiming descent through his mother from Edward III. But the poet's father, mysteriously thrust aside by *his* father in favour of a younger brother, and destined for holy orders (from the early age, apparently, of twelve), grew up a handsome, gifted, and learned man, yet eccentric, melancholy, and understandably bitter with the bitterness of Esau.[1] He appears to have lived out his days like a storm-tossed yew-tree, impressive, but awesome and forbidding.

Into his Somersby rectory were crammed eleven children, as well as numerous servants. Of his seven sons, all wrote verse, three became recognized poets, but all were, like their father, eccentric; one was to take temporarily to opium, one to alcohol, one to go out of his mind.[2] The household darkened as Dr Tennyson grew yet gloomier, gave way to drinking, and became mentally dangerous; while his wife, once beautiful,[3] always simple and devout, was bowed under her burdens. Still one should not exaggerate the gloom; 'The Devil and the Lady', written by Alfred at fourteen, bubbles at times with gaiety. All the same there were days when the boy would lie among the graves in Somersby churchyard, wishing he too were dead. Cambridge provided a temporary escape; it brought him the friendship of Hallam, the admiration of the undergraduate society of 'Apostles', the growing realization of his genius. But his father died; he was withdrawn from the University; his poetry was savaged by critics; Hallam, betrothed to his

[1] An old housekeeper is said to have described him as lying abed till three or four in the afternoon; or 'glowering' in his study, its walls covered 'wi' 'eathen gods and goddesses wi'out cloäs'.

[2] Compare Tennyson's own remark: 'I am black-blooded like all the Tennysons'; and the observation of his brother Septimus, as he rose lankly from a prostrate position on the hearthrug at the Hallams' house in Wimpole Street, and introduced himself to an astonished visitor—'I am Septimus, the *most* morbid of the Tennysons'.

[3] She had received twenty-five proposals of marriage.

sister, died suddenly in Vienna. His own engagement, a few years later, was broken off for a whole decade. Only with his 1842 volume, his pension (1845), his marriage and Laureateship (1850), did his fortune change and at last set fair.

Still, many men have fared far worse. Yet happiness depends, as a rule, less on circumstance than on temperament. And here we come to that complex melancholy which is fundamental to the understanding of Tennyson.

As in Matthew Arnold the Hebrew waged lifelong war with the Hellene, so too in Tennyson there appears a double character, with a stronger and harsher, a softer and weaker side. On the one hand there is the impressive Tennyson, tall, gipsy-dark, often as unkempt as his style was polished, strikingly handsome in youth, awesome as a Hebrew prophet in his bearded age; the young Hercules who tossed iron bars over haystacks, or carried ponies round lawns, who seemed to FitzGerald 'a sort of Hyperion', and to a later observer 'a dilapidated Jove', to Carlyle 'a Life-guardsman spoilt by making poetry', and to Sydney Dobell a figure capable of composing *The Iliad* itself; with senses so vivid that he could hear a bat shriek and, though myopic, glimpse the moon reflected in a nightingale's eye; with such vitality that even at seventy-seven he had not a grey hair in his mane;[1] yet often gruff and formidable,[2] liking his meat in wedges, his tea in bowls, his tobacco in two-gallon jars enjoying clay pipes, public-house port, and broad stories; often grim in his humour, so that he would shake with sardonic laughter in reading his own 'St Simeon', or indulge

---

[1] He was annoyed at being identified with the 'old white-headed dreamer' of *Locksley Hall Sixty Years After*: 'I that have not a white hair on my head!'

[2] This side of him came out remarkably when, by the kindness of Sir Charles Tennyson, I heard the old poet read some of his own verse. The readings were recorded on a primitive type of phonograph; and their effect was the reverse of that honeysuckle sweetness some associate with Tennyson—it suggested, rather, a rugged old countryman. 'Blow, bugle, blow,' which *could* be imagined a slightly sentimental little lyric, was growled out as if it were sounding a charge; and 'Come into the garden, Maud' assumed tones at which Maud could only have trembled and obeyed.

in strange impersonations of the toad-shaped Satan whispering in the ear of Eve, or a cannibal chief inspecting edible missionaries; Johnsonian, at times, in his ruthless downrightness;[1] yet, like Johnson, noble, generous, compassionate amid his melancholia.

This was the Tennyson that impressed widely diverse minds like Carlyle, Thackeray, FitzGerald, George Eliot, Jowett, and Gladstone, as no mellifluous mediocrity could have done—the Olympian before whose sombre dignity captious critics seem petulantly impertinent: '*They* do it wrong, being so Majesticall.'

But with this Tennyson there was coupled a strange sort of anti-self—shy, self-concious, hysterical, hyper-sensitive to criticism as the legendary princess to the pea beneath ten mattresses[2]; the 'school-miss Alfred' of Lytton's satire and of verse like 'The Darling Room'; soft as the south winds of spring across the Isle of Wight.

[1] This is best illustrated by some of his recorded utterances.

(To a young lady at dinner, who had described a marriage as 'penniless'; slamming a penny on the tablecloth.) 'There!—I give you that, for that is the god you worship.'

(To extravagant homage from Mrs Greville.) 'Oh yes, you may do what you like—so long as you don't kiss me in front of the cabman.'

(To a small, nervous Eton master, prattling at him in a high wind.)'I don't know who you are, and I can't hear what you say.'

(To a member of the Royal Family, who had forced him to read her a poem.) 'There you are, and I don't suppose you've understood a word of it.'

(To Hubert Parry, using the phrase 'awfully good'.) 'I'd sooner you said "bloody".'

(To Gosse, inquiring how he was.) 'Old and ugly, old and ugly.'

(To Oscar Browning, introducing himself at a party with the words: 'I'm Browning'; after a myopic stare.) 'No, you're not!'

Compare his comment on *Sordello*, that he had only understood the first line and the last, and *they* were lies; on the Carlyles' marriage, that it was better two people should be miserable than four; and on Churton Collins, the critic—'a louse on the locks of literature'.

This is not a side of Tennyson familiar in the Victorian Age, nor even now. A pity—for it is far more human.

[2] 'In my youth the growls!
In mine age the owls!
After death the ghouls!'

One can, if one likes, link the tougher-minded of these two personalities with Tennyson's father, the stern doctor; and the tender-minded one with his gentle, pietistic mother; yet it is hazardous guessing about heredity. It might also seem temptingly simple to attribute Tennyson's enduring work to the masculine side of him, his ephemeral verse to the feminine. But it is safer to say only that it was *as if* he had two different persons in him, sometimes conflicting, sometimes collaborating. Possibly he even gained from this two-sidedness; for it may well be that Wordsworth, for example, suffered from a certain lack of femininity. Still, I suspect that where Tennyson's feminine side grew dominant, his poetry suffered; and that, in later years, his sheltered life in southern England helped to bring out that weaker side.

On the other hand, it is fair to remember that this gentler voice of Tennyson, though it maundered at moments into a fearsome falsetto, has also left us much of grace and melody.

> And on her lover's arm she leant,
>   And round her waist she felt it fold,
> And far across the hills they went
>   In that new world which is the old:
> Across the hills, and far away
>   Beyond their utmost purple rim,
> And deep into the dying day
>   The happy princess follow'd him.
>
> ('The Day-dream')

> Once more the Heavenly Power
>   Makes all things new,
> And domes the red-plow'd hills
>   With loving blue;
> The blackbirds have their wills,
>   The throstles too . . .
>
> O follow, leaping blood,
>   The season's lure!

> O heart, look down and up,
>   Serene, secure,
> Warm as the crocus cup,
>   Like snowdrops, pure!

('Early Spring')

Let us not despise the day of such small things, like some
modern writers and critics who have tongues as rasping as
cats, and seem to think that the first thing in art is to be
disagreeable. Let us thank Heaven for Herrick and La
Fontaine, as well as for Webster and Baudelaire. Still it
remains true, as Yeats put it, that 'though it is charming to
have an affectionate feeling for flowers, that will not pull
the cart out of the ditch'. And though life, fortunately, does
not wholly consist in pulling carts out of ditches, none the
less if one would see Tennyson, not only as a charming poet,
but as a grand one, it becomes necessary to turn back to that
harsher side of him with its bitterness, its anger, and its
gloom. To hear his utterance at its deepest, one must see
him, like Hamlet, in the presence of his stern father's ghost—
that ghost which he vainly hoped to see when he slept, on
the night of his father's burial, in his father's bed at Somersby.

> 'Consider well,' the voice replied,
> 'His face, that two hours since hath died;
>   Wilt thou find passion, pain or pride? . . .
>
> 'High up the vapours fold and swim:
> About him broods the twilight dim:
>   The place he knew forgetteth him . . .
>
> 'A life of nothings, nothing-worth,
> From that first nothing ere his birth
>   To that last nothing under earth!
>
> 'From when his baby pulses beat
> To when his hands in their last heat
>   Pluck at the death-mote in the sheet.'[1]

('The Two Voices')

[1] Tennyson's father died in 1831; the poem dates from 1833. The last
stanza here quoted was not published, as too macabre.

Come not, when I am dead,
   To drop thy foolish tears upon my grave,
To trample round my fallen head,
   And vex the unhappy dust thou wouldst not save.
There let the wind sweep and the plover cry;
   But thou, go by.[1]

                   ('Come not, when I am dead')

    'Wine is good for shrivell'd lips,
       When a blanket wraps the day,
   When the rotten woodland drips,
       And the leaf is stamp'd in clay . . .

    'Virtue!—to be good and just—
       Every heart, when sifted well,
   Is a clot of warmer dust,
       Mix'd with cunning sparks of hell . . .

    'Fill the can, and fill the cup:
       All the windy ways of men
   Are but dust that rises up,
       And is lightly laid again.'

                   ('The Vision of Sin')

The moanings of the homeless sea,
   The sound of streams that swift or slow
   Draw down Aeonian hills, and sow
The dust of continents to be . . .

Be near me when the sensuous frame
   Is rack'd with pangs that conquer trust;
   And Time, a maniac scattering dust,
And Life, a Fury slinging flame . . .

'So careful of the type?' But no.
   From scarped cliff and quarried stone
   She cries, 'A thousand types are gone:
I care for nothing, all shall go.'

                      (*In Memoriam*)

[1] Lines that the first Mrs Meredith, parted from her husband, wished put on her tomb.

Dear as remember'd kisses after death,
And sweet as those by hopeless fancy feign'd
On lips that are for others; deep as love,
Deep as first love, and wild with all regret;
O Death in Life, the days that are no more.

('Tears, idle tears'[1] in *The Princess*)

Comfort? comfort scorn'd of devils! this is truth the poet sings,
That a sorrow's crown of sorrow is remembering happier things.

Drug thy memories, lest thou learn it, lest thy heart be put to proof,
In the dead unhappy night, and when the rain is on the roof.

('Locksley Hall')

Coldly thy rosy shadows bathe me, cold
Are all thy lights, and cold my wrinkled feet
Upon thy glimmering thresholds, when the steam
Floats up from those dim fields about the homes
Of happy men that have the power to die,
And grassy barrows of the happier dead.

('Tithonus')

Even as I copy these, I feel for the hundredth time what a
superb poet Tennyson, at his best, could be—passion, sense,
clarity, music; not a word wasted, not a stroke blurred, not
a tone out of tune. When gay, he can be charming; but,
when gloomy, he can become great. It is his too solemn
moments of uplift that fall flat today; his attempts at senti-
ment that fail to make us feel.

III

The critic who reaches this conclusion, that Tennyson's
darkest hours were often his finest, must ask himself whether
such a judgement may not merely be a personal prejudice in
favour of pessimism. But I do not think it is simply that.
Chaucer, for example, seems to me to succeed best when he

[1] Even Carlyle, with all his scorn for 'jingling', was known to quote
from this.

is gayest—in 'The Nun's Priest's Tale' rather than in 'The Knight's Tale'; in 'The House of Fame' rather than in 'The Book of the Duchess'. With tragic horrors like the hunger-tower of Pisa, where Dante grows terrible, Chaucer, I feel, tends to fail. *Candide*, again, seems to me to succeed better than the sadder *Rasselas*; and, in general, the melancholy Johnson becomes most enthralling, not in his moods of inspissated gloom, but when he is vigorously tossing and goring his acquaintances, or laughing like a rhinoceros. The trouble is, that when Tennyson tries to break out of his genuine unhappiness, the edifying consolations he clutches at are apt to seem straws; the 'larger hope' tends to ring false; so that some readers find themselves recalling the anguished cry of Clough:

> I tremble for something factitious
> Some malpractice of heart, some illegitimate process.

'*In Memoriam*', Tennyson is reported to have said, 'is more optimistic than I am.' It may well be that the mood where Tennyson was most spontaneously himself, and not battling desperately to become something different, was, rather, the mood of 'Tithonus'. At all events, to his poetry in general, one may not unjustly apply that verse of Alfred de Musset: *Les plus désespérés sont les chants les plus beaux.*[1]

Plato, no doubt, might have objected that the poetry of sorrow and despair is futile, and worse than futile, since it unmans mankind. But that view seems over-simple. When Andromache, Hecuba, and Helen lament above Hector dead, the bitterness of death may seem to grow bitterer still; and yet there is consolation in the beauty of their poetry.

[1] Contrast the typically Victorian criticism which half amused, half enraged Tennyson in 1851: 'We exhort Mr. Tennyson to abandon the weeping willow with its fragile and earthward pointing twigs, and adopt the poplar, with its one heavenward pointing finger'; or Carlyle's description of him, in the same year, as 'sitting on a dung-heap among innumerable dead dogs' (though, when taxed with it by Tennyson years afterwards, Carlyle admitted it was not 'a very luminous description').

And again, as Aristotle saw, the very violence of the grief aroused may leave behind it the calm of passsion spent. So with the lamentations of the Muses, age after age, over human life itself. The hideousness of the face of fate may seem half redeemed by the nobility of the faces that confront it. And among those mourning Muses no mean place belongs to Tennyson's.

Perhaps a truer objection might be that, though his best poetry is tragic, it is not the best kind of tragic poetry, because often too passive, too inert. Homer is tragic; yet what poetry was ever fuller of action? One may wonder whether, if Tennyson had sailed with Odysseus, he might not have been one of those too quick despairers who abandoned themselves to stay with the Lotos-eaters. When Tennyson fell in love, he waited patiently, but somewhat passively, for fourteen years, till Fate at last gave him his desire: when Arnold fell in love, he promptly turned inspector of schools to win his Rachel—not that he had any love for inspecting schools; but he loved *her*.

Arnold's 'Sohrab and Rustum' is tragic; but it is active tragedy. As Arnold said, 'it animates'. Tennyson's 'Tithonus' is a marvellous lament; but it is passive. That may be less healthy. For most modern critics, I know, such a quality does not so much as exist. But that need not make it less real.

This is, of course, only one quality among many. I am not proposing to put Macaulay and Kipling above Wordsworth. To 'Sohrab and Rustum' many, unlike Arnold himself, may still prefer 'The Scholar Gipsy' or 'Thyrsis', though they are not tragically active, but elegiacally passive. And I own that I prefer 'Tithonus' to 'Ulysses', although the spirit of 'Ulysses' breathes more energy—because 'Tithonus' seems to me more genuinely true to the spirit of Tennyson himself, who showed little impulse towards voyaging in strange seas, till his hour came to 'cross the bar'.

The tragic Tennyson, in fact, is more like one of those grave elders in a Greek Chorus who meditate and mourn, as passive spectators, over the lot of man.

Never to born is best;
Next to that, far happiest
He that hastens from his birth,
Fast as may be, back to earth.[1]

This kind of contemplative poetry can stand, no doubt, very high—only not quite, I think, with the highest. Tennyson's verse might have gained still greater strength, had he been more of an actor in life, less of a choric looker-on. He remains a fascinatingly interesting personality; but perhaps with a touch too much of Hamlet (just as he called his own 'Maud' 'a little Hamlet').

The theme of his 'Palace of Art' is that a man should not try to live in art. Conscience transforms the palace to a hell. But instead of turning to the active world like Goethe's Faust, Tennyson's Soul only exchanges one retirement for another, an ivory tower for an ivory cottage, 'where I may mourn and pray'. Not a very potent conclusion. The Lady of Shalott similarly grows 'sick of shadows', like Ibsen's sculptor in *When We Dead Awaken*. But her entry into active reality takes only the passive form of floating dead down a river in a boat (which would have grounded in the reeds long before it reached Camelot[2]).

One may wish, in fine, that Tennyson could have been more like a Greek poet writing poetry in the intervals of agora and battlefield; or like Chaucer, by turns soldier, diplomat, courtier, customs-officer, administrator, Member of Parliament. Browning, indeed, regretted in later life that he had not been, also, a civil servant—'I have written too much, my dear Mr. Gosse; I have over-written; I have written myself out.' I am not clear that it was at all a good thing for literature when it became, in the late seventeenth century, a profession.

Such, at all events, was the conviction of FitzGerald. And among all contemporary critics of Tennyson, it is to Fitz-Gerald that I find myself constantly returning for real sense

[1] Sophocles, *Oedipus at Colonus*, 1224–7.
[2] Elaine, more prudently, employed an old oarsman.

and truth. He wrote no formal criticism of the friend he loved, yet lamented over: he simply wrote from his heart in private letters. And that is a great advantage.

Of the 1842 poems:

But with all his faults, he will publish such a volume as has not been published since the time of Keats: and which, once published, will never be suffered to die. (1842)

Why reprint the Merman, the Mermaid, and those everlasting Eleanores, Isabels?—which always were, and are, and must be, a nuisance, though Mrs. Butler (who recognized herself in the portrait, of course) said that Eleanore (what a bore) was the finest thing he ever wrote. She has sat for it ever since, I believe. (1842)

Of *In Memoriam*, obviously seen in MS:

I felt that if Tennyson had got on a horse & ridden 20 miles, instead of moaning over his pipe, he would have been cured of his sorrows in half the time. As it is, it is about 3 years before the Poetic Soul walks itself out of darkness & Despair into Common Sense—Plato w^d not have allowed such querulousness to be published in his Republic, to be sure: and when we think of the Miss Barretts, Brownes, Jewsburys &c who will set to work to feel friends' losses in melodious tears, in imitation of A.T's—one must allow Plato was no such prig as some say he was. (1845)

To E. B. Cowell:

It came upon me 'come stella in ciel', when in the account of the taking of Amphipolis, Thucydides, [who wrote this history,] comes with 7 ships to the rescue! ... This was the way to write well. ... Oh, Alfred Tennyson, could you but have the luck to be put to such employment! No man would do it better; a more heroic figure to head the defenders of his country could not be. (1848)

Of *In Memoriam*:

It is full of the finest things, but it is monotonous, and has that air of being evolved by a Poetical Machine of the highest order. ... It is the cursed inactivity (very pleasant to me who am no Hero) of this 19th century which has spoiled Alfred, I mean spoiled him for the great work he ought now to be entering upon; the lovely and noble things he has done must remain. (1850)

Of Lady Tennyson:

She is a graceful lady, but I think that she and other aesthetic and hysterical Ladies have hurt A.T., who, *quoad* Artist, would have done better to remain single in Lincolnshire, or married a jolly Woman who would have laughed and cried without any reason why. But this is foolish and wicked Talking. (1864)

To Tennyson, on the 'Holy Grail' volume:

I am not sure if the old knights' adventures do not tell upon me better, touched in some lyrical way (like your own 'Lady of Shalott') than when elaborated into epic form. . . . I read on till the 'Lincolnshire Farmer' drew tears to my eyes. I was got back to the substantial rough-spun Nature I knew; and the old brute, invested by you with the solemn humour of Humanity, like Shakespeare's *Shallow*, became a more pathetic phenomenon than the knights who revisit the world in your other verse. (1870)

To Fanny Kemble:

When Tennyson was telling me of how the *Quarterly* abused him (humorously too), and desirous of knowing why one did not care for his later works, etc., I thought if he had lived an active life as Scott and Shakespeare; or even ridden, shot, drunk, and played the Devil, as Byron, he would have done much more, and talked about it much less. 'You know,' said Scott to Lockhart, 'that I don't care a Curse about what I write,' and one sees he did not. I don't believe it was far otherwise with Shakespeare. Even old Wordsworth, wrapt up in his Mountain mists, and proud as he was, was above all this vain Disquietude. (1876)

Partly, no doubt, from temperament, but partly also, I suspect, because of the shy and sheltered life he chose, Tennyson, though himself a remarkable character, was not as a rule able to create remarkable characters, as Chaucer could, or Shakespeare, or the great nineteenth-century novelists. Like Browning, he wrote plays, tales, monologues; but, like Browning, he seems to get, not into the skins of his characters, but only into their shoes. Shakespeare's Caliban is—Caliban: but Browning's Caliban remains Browning as he might have been, if born a hairy primitive. Tennyson's Tithonus or Lucretius is Tennyson in Greek tunic or Roman toga. Doubtless there are exceptions, like Browning's Bishop of St Praxed's, or Tennyson's Lincolnshire rustics, based on his boyhood's memories; but both poets seem to me essentially lyric, not epic or dramatic.

Still it is graceless, where so much is given, to grumble for more. After all, very few English poets have ever been able to write a play (except at one brief period), or to tell a story. The way to enjoy Tennyson is to look to him for what he is—a superb landscape-painter, a consummate musician. With his technical genius and patience, he is in some sort (though a far finer person) the Alexander Pope of Romanticism.

For example, he wrote (typical title) 'A Dream of Fair Women'; but the fair women remain dream-figures; it is their setting that lives. So with his many heroines mourning for lost loves—he had a passion for them—the two Marianas, the two Oenones, the Lady of Shalott, the Maid of Astolat, Guinevere. Even if Oenone may be only a painted grief upon a painted mountain—yet what painting! What we remember is that valley of Ionian hills, the mist that snakes athwart the pines of Ida, the blue abysses of its gorges, the dazzling white of peak and cataract, the whirl of reedy Simois. Tennyson's Mariana is hardly more a human person than his Dying Swan amid its equal desolation; what endures is that picture of black moss, black fenland-waters, black levels of sodden plain beneath the grey glint of dawn, the dance of motes in the sinking sunlight, the white curtains wavering beneath the setting moon, the poplar-shadow across the forsaken bed. The theme of 'The Lady of Shalott' is like many a play of Ibsen's—a sheltered, secluded, unreal life, lit up and shattered suddenly by the lightning of reality. Instead of the breathing, tortured creatures of Ibsen there are only a phantom Lady, a Lancelot like a knight in tapestry; and yet what colours, such as Ibsen never dreamed!

The gemmy bridle glitter'd free,
Like to some branch of stars we see
Hung in the golden Galaxy.
The bridle bells rang merrily
        As he rode down to Camelot:
And from his blazon'd baldric slung
A mighty silver bugle hung,
And as he rode his armour rung
        Beside remote Shalott.

Similarly with that other series of poems, equally Tenny-sonian, where it is a man, left lonely, that mourns a mistress lost. 'Love and Duty' is a poignant memory of his own enforced parting from Emily Sellwood. It is the tragedy of Virgil's Dido and Aeneas, of Racine's Titus and Berenice. Yet, despite the autobiography, the figures seem unreal; till all at once the poem springs to life as it breathes its last, and on its vague Victorian sentiments there strikes the light of dawn:

Then when the first low matin-chirp hath grown
Full quire, and mourning driv'n her plow of pearl
Far furrowing into light the mounded rack,
Beyond the fair green field and eastern sea.

As for the heroes of 'Locksley Hall' and 'Maud', even that son of exaggeration, Swinburne, exaggerated rather less than usual when he wrote, in one of his frenzies of alliteration: 'It cannot respectfully be supposed that Lord Tennyson is unaware of the paltry currishness and mean-spirited malice displayed in verse too dainty for such base uses by the plaintively spiteful manikins, with the thinnest whey of sour milk in their poor fretful veins, whom he brings forward to vent upon some fickle or too discerning mistress the vain and languid venom of their contemptible contempt.' Nor is the disillusioned modern reader necessarily much delighted by prophecies of grappling air-fleets or of the Federation of the World. What lasts, yet again, in 'Locksley Hall' is the vision of natural beauty, of the unchanging hosts of Heaven:

'Tis the place, and all around it, as of old, the curlews call,
Dreary gleams about the moorland flying over Locksley Hall . . .

Many a night from yonder ivied casement, ere I went to rest,
Did I look on great Orion sloping slowly to the West.

Many a night I saw the Pleiads, rising through the mellow shade,
Glitter like a swarm of fire-flies tangled in a silver braid.

So in 'Maud'. The melodrama drags; yet coming out of
the great house into the garden, how we revive! (It is often
as if the gipsy in Tennyson breathed most happily out of
doors.)

> Come into the garden, Maud,
>   For the black bat, night, has flown,
> Come into the garden, Maud,
>   I am here at the gate alone;
> And the woodbine spices are wafted abroad,
>   And the musk of the rose is blown . . .
>
> All night have the roses heard
>   The flute, violin, bassoon;
> All night has the casement jessamine stirr'd
>   To the dancers dancing in tune;
> Till a silence fell with the wakening bird,
>   And a hush with the setting moon.[1]

'Tithonus' is, for me, the most splendid thing Tennyson
ever wrote. It does not matter that its aged hero is less alive
than even the dying leaves of autumn:

> The woods decay, the woods decay and fall,
> The vapours weep their burthen to the ground,
> Man comes and tills the field and lies beneath,
> And after many a summer dies the swan.
> Me only cruel immortality
> Consumes: I wither slowly in thine arms,
> Here at the quiet limit of the world,

[1] Margot Asquith records that, after reading aloud part of this section
of 'Maud', 'he pulled me on to his knee and said: "Many have written as
well as that, but nothing that ever sounded so well".' Vain; but one can
forgive it.

A white-hair'd shadow roaming like a dream
The ever-silent spaces of the East,
Far-folded mists, and gleaming halls of morn.[1]

It does not matter that Eos, who loved him once, is less human still; for never was dawn more divine.

Thy cheek begins to redden thro' the gloom,
Thy sweet eyes brighten slowly close to mine,
Ere yet they blind the stars, and the wild team
Which love thee, yearning for thy yoke, arise
And shake the darkness from their loosen'd manes,
And beat the twilight into flakes of fire.

It does not matter that no decrepit ancient, shrivelled almost to a grasshopper, could be conceived bursting into vigour so magnificent. Who cares?

Enoch Arden conquered Germany, when Germany was still sentimental. But today that worthy fisherman keeps no such vitality as the Peter Grimes of Crabbe; the poem subsists only by its riot of tropic landscape, its bleak English winter-day with the robin piping from a dead-leaved tree. So, I feel, with 'Aylmer's Field'; so even with *The Princess*; so even with *In Memoriam*. The hero of that poem too (once irritably dismissed by *The Times* as 'an Amaryllis of the Chancery Bar') remains a wraith—as nebulous as Edward King in 'Lycidas', or Clough in 'Thyrsis'; the philosophy, for

[1] Aldous Huxley commented: 'Why the swan? Heaven knows. The swan is a luminous irrelevance, sailing for a moment into the picture with all its curves and its whiteness and its mythologies, and sailing out again to the strains of a defunctive music, fabulously mournful. Tennyson knew his magician's business.' This is beautifully said; but it seems to me typical of much modern criticism. Our Byzantinism loves far-fetched explanations better than common sense; and many of us, being jaded, or impatient, think irrelevance a virtue. But in 1833 irrelevance was not yet a virtue. The point of the swan is quite simple: (1) Aristotle, Aelian, and Gesner credit the swan with extreme longevity ('some say 300 years'); (2) the white swan is an ancient symbol of white-haired age: e.g. an epigram of Martial addresses a gentleman who has dyed his hair—'What!—turned a crow! Just now you were a swan.' Tennyson understood his magician's business well enough—but he understood it differently.

many readers, flaps its ineffectual way along a vale of tears;[1]
yet one never tires of the rooks whirled headlong in the
stormy sunlight above the autumn trees, the sombre yew in
the churchyard with the faint gold of springtime in its tips,
the blank London dawn on the drizzle of Wimpole Street,
the silver fingers of the moonlight stealing along the letters
of Hallam's name in Clevedon Church beside the Severn
sea, the moonbeams flashing arrowlike on the brook by the
forsaken home at Somersby, or the dawn-wind of yet
another Tennysonian dawn:

> And suck'd from out the distant gloom
> A breeze began to tremble o'er
> The large leaves of the sycamore,
> And fluctuate all the still perfume,
>
> And gathering freshlier overhead,
> Rock'd the full-foliaged elms, and swung
> The heavy-folded rose, and flung
> The lilies to and fro, and said
>
> 'The dawn, the dawn', and died away;
> And East and West, without a breath,
> Mixt their dim lights, like life and death,
> To broaden into boundless day.

Once the *Idylls of the King* crowned Tennyson's fame:
today men would rather blame them than read them. Yet
perhaps they miss more than they realize. The *dramatis per-
sonae* may often seem puppets; yet, here too, the scene-
painting is often consummate—as when Bleys and Merlin
snatch the infant Arthur from the great phosphorescent
wave upon Tintagel shore; or Gareth comes, amid the

---

[1] For example:
> He fought his doubts and gather'd strength,
> He would not make his judgment blind.

To some the second line will seem to contradict the first.
> A warmth within the breast would melt
> The freezing reason's colder part,
> And like a man in wrath the heart
> Stood up and answer'd 'I have felt'.

But so, precisely, Hitler might have said.

myriad pine-tops, on that lonely mere glaring in the sunset, 'round as the red eye of an Eagle-owl'; or in the ruined castle of Enid's girlhood the knotted snakes of ivy climb sucking the mortar from its shattered towers; or Merlin dimly sees his doom like the white wavecrest mirrored in the glassy sand beneath it as it breaks; or in the misty moonlight of a glen in Lyonnesse the King treads from its skeleton a skull with jewelled crown; or Lancelot drifts across the moonlit surf to the lion-haunted tower of Carbonek. Over the fallen head of Guinevere once George Eliot wept, and Swinburne stormed; but today one turns, instead, to watch that white mist creeping over the wintry earth under the hidden moon, or in the torch-glare at Almesbury—

> Wet with the mists and smitten by the lights,
> The Dragon of the great Pendragonship
> Blaze, making all the night a steam of fire.

We may watch dry-eyed, now, the passing of Arthur; yet there is still life in that seascape of the days when first he came:

> All down the lonely coast of Lyonnesse,
> Each with a beacon-star upon his head,
> And with a wild sea-light about his feet,
> He saw them—headland after headland flame
> Far on into the rich heart of the west:
> And in the light the white mermaiden swam,
> And strong man-breasted things stood from the sea,
> And sent a deep sea-voice through all the land.

And there is still life, no less, in that bitterly contrasting sea-scape of the last wreckage of the Table Round:

> Only the wan wave
> Brake in among dead faces, to and fro
> Swaying the helpless hands, and up and down
> Tumbling the hollow helmets of the fallen,
> And shiver'd brands that once had fought with Rome,
> And rolling far along the gloomy shores
> The voice of days of old and days to be.

If it be objected, 'then the *Idylls* are mainly things of golden shreds and purple patches', then I cannot deny it. Indeed that is my point. Yet the gold is often burnished, and the purple royal.

IV

Tennyson, like Johnson, remains one of the most English of English writers. Hence to the foreign reader his qualities may often seem elusive. Taine misconceived him; Verlaine, having thought of translating him, decided he was 'too English, too noble'. He is full of English traits that are sometimes virtues, sometimes defects, sometimes both—often insular; often egotistic; eccentric, yet conventional; rude, yet touchy; sentimental, yet gruff; humorous, yet melancholy; tender-hearted, but muddle-headed; thoughtful, but too fond of half-thoughts and half-measures, with what the exasperated Marx called our 'mania for compromise and thirst for respectability'. But no poet has caught with clearer eye and ear that quiet beauty (which we are rapidly doing our best to destroy) of English landscape, sky, and sea—a beauty that does not strive nor cry; infinitely various and loveable, though seldom stupendous or cataclysmic. And few writers (though some have found him over-careful and elaborate) have used with such melody and purity the English tongue.

Tennyson could hardly have become a world-writer—acted in Moscow like Shakespeare, or read in Russia like Dickens. Not only was he somewhat insular—or, in Arnold's phrase, 'provincial'; not only did he fail to create crowds of vivid characters which other races could re-create, partly in their own image; it is also hard for a foreigner to feel fully his painting of English landscape, the pure music of his English style—just as an Englishman wonders how a Frenchman finds such beauty in the style of Racine, or fails to feel the defects of style in Byron or in Poe.

Yet there may be much in the idea of Yeats that a writer *ought* to be provincial—rooted in his own corner of the earth, not a drifting, vague cosmopolite. (Just as Hardy was rooted in his Wessex.) No doubt, its wide diversity has been, and is, a weakness for Europe; as once it was for Greece. Yet, as with Greece, this diversity has also been of vital value. For Europe has gained from its variety of landscape and human types a stimulus that is lacking in the monotony of more uniform expanses of the earth. There can be danger, as well as hope, in the obliteration of national differences. There has been too much of it already. The heart sinks at the vision of a world where every country girl from Galway to Tokyo should ape the modes of Paris, and breathe the dreams of Hollywood. That Tennyson is in many ways so English, can make him more, not less, interesting to the intelligent foreigner. We too may be worth knowing—difficult though we sometimes make it.

Further, he had qualities that belong, not to this nation or to that, but to humanity at its best. In his admirable biography of his grandfather Sir Charles Tennyson records that, just before the Second War, 'an acute young critic', being asked what he thought greatest in Tennyson, replied: 'Tennyson will always rank among the first, because he is the most human of the great poets.' I distrust prophecies: I distrust superlatives. There are many other poets who might be thought no less human—Homer, Euripides, Virgil, Horace, Po-chu-i, Hafiz, Chaucer, Ronsard, Shakespeare, Morris, Hardy . . . Still the judgement is interesting; and helps to justify, I think, the stress I have laid on Tennyson's personality. Humane, and humanist, he was; but perhaps his special power was, rather, to feel better than most, and to express far better than most, that sense of natural beauty which needs today more than ever to be cherished if man is not to decline into a species of mechanized termite—*formicanthropus insipiens*. At the same time, though the sensitive may grow over-delicate and aesthetes have often become decadent, Tennyson remained fundamentally sane and sound. Verlaine found him 'too English'; but Verlaine's comment, when the Prussians marched on Paris, was merely, 'Now we shall have some decent music'; Tennyson would not have said that in 1940. There are drawbacks to decadence. I suspect that in his later years Taine might have done Tennyson more justice; for it is told that, when sickened with study of the corruptions of the *ancien régime*, Taine would refresh himself by going and gazing at a sturdy little tree in a courtyard of Les Invalides—here at least was *'un être bien portant'*. Tennyson too, despite the burdens of his heredity and childhood, contrived to become, in essentials, *'un être bien portant'*. Would there were more modern writers of whom that could be said!

Open a collected *Tennyson* at the first poem:

> At eve the beetle boometh
> Athwart the thicket lone:
> At noon the wild bee hummeth
> About the moss'd headstone:
> At midnight the moon cometh
> And looketh down alone.

('Claribel')

Claribel herself is a mere wraith, among the vaguest even of Tennyson's dream-women, far fainter than even the Sylph of Chateaubriand's young imaginings. She is dead without ever having lived. Some might find the poem mawkish: some might find it precious, with its lisping -eths. What stands forth is, again, its background—lonely thicket, wild bee, booming beetle, and that moon which, sixty years later, was to look down alone on the dying poet himself, with his Shakespeare in his hand. For half a century these have hummed, and boomed, and glimmered at moments in my memory.

Now turn to his final page:

> But such a tide as moving seems asleep,
> Too full for sound and foam,
> When that which drew from out the boundless deep
> Turns again home. . . .

For tho' from out our bourne of Time and Place
The flood may bear me far,
I hope to see my Pilot face to face
When I have crost the bar.

('Crossing the Bar')

A metaphysical German mind might cavil at the naïve anthropomorphism of attributing to the Absolute a 'face'.[1] A sceptically logical French one might question this trust in a pilotry that has strewn the shores of life, since its first creation, with the wreckage of pain and death—did not the youth who lifted, in the legend, the veil from the face of Isis, die of horror at what lay behind? The 'home' of the Atlantic tides is, after all, only a desolate welter of inhuman waters, cold-eyed monsters, and black abysses without end. And yet even the unconvinced and unconverted, who might wish this last stanza away, must surely marvel at the poetic gift which, even at eighty, could so well see and feel and utter the resistless majesty of that midnight tide, 'too full for sound and foam'.

When all is said, has any poet, since Aeschylus composed his own epitaph, paid so fine a farewell to life? (For Browning's valediction seems perhaps a trifle boastful; Landor's, a little arrogant; Housman's, a little ambiguous.)

Much that was idolized in Tennyson by his own age, has passed with it; but 'though much is taken, much abides'—a poet of whom Housman, never lavish with incense, could write that there was no one in English poetry, except Shakespeare himself, who had produced 'excellent things so diverse in their excellence'.

Poets, like other men, may be divided into the tender-minded and the tough. The tough are apt to despise the tender. Yet, if tenderness can grow degenerate, toughness can grow barbarous. Mankind needs both. Tennyson, like Virgil, is the compassionate poet of a Golden Age. True, even Golden Ages are heavily alloyed. Even under Augustus

---

[1] Tennyson, of course, could have retorted that it was merely a metaphor —an apt echo of St Paul.

and Victoria groaned millions in their misery. And Golden Ages are brief, like the golden days of an English summer, when the world seems perfect, yet the next depression is already labouring up past the Azores. So, behind Virgil's world and behind Tennyson's, we can hear now the tramp of marching barbarians. And when Alaric stands before Rome, or Hitler at Dunkirk, the hour is gone for pastoral pipings, and the most majestic melancholy will not help. The only valid mood becomes that of Morris's Icelanders:

> But if nor Christ, nor Odin help, why, then
> Still at the worst are we the sons of men.

As an answer to life and death that, for me, rings truer than Tennyson—even the Tennyson of *The Revenge*. And so it becomes easy for our tormented century to growl at him, as Carlyle did, for providing only 'superlative lollipops'; or as Arnold did, for 'dawdling with life's painted shell'. Yet such harshness, carried far enough, would lead to the negation of all civilization, all grace, all art. Men have need also of happier dreams. At times they may even come true. After all, there is truth in the Chinese paradox that soft and delicate things can prove stronger, in the end, than hard, as the tongue outlasts the teeth, and water outwears the rock. Even through the Dark Ages men remembered Virgil. Our own age has its shadows. Like savages, we are befouling the natural beauty of the world; like rabbits, we are recklessly overcrowding it. But one may still dream—however many centuries away—of a different world, with population drastically reduced, where human quality replaces the horrible human quantity of today, and there is room again for that natural beauty of the much-loved earth which poets like Theocritus and Virgil, Wordsworth and Tennyson have made lovelier still.

TENNYSON

A Select Bibliography

(Place of publication London, unless stated otherwise. Detailed biblio-graphical information will also be found in the appropriate volume of *The Cambridge Bibliography of English Literature*).

Bibliography:

A BIBLIOGRAPHY OF THE WRITINGS OF TENNYSON, by T. J. W[ise], 2 vols. Privately printed, 1908
—see also Wise's *The Ashley Library*, vol. VII.

BIBLIOGRAPHIES OF TWELVE VICTORIAN AUTHORS, by T. G. Ehrsam and R. H. Deily, New York (1936).

Note: Tennyson's MS Notebooks and loose sheets, containing at least partial drafts of all his most important poems except 'Locksley Hall', are in the Houghton Library at Harvard. The final holograph of *In Memoriam* is in the Library of Trinity College, Cambridge. T. J. Wise's great Tennyson collection, including many trial and privately printed editions (and his own forgeries), is in the Ashley Library in the British Museum.

Collected Works:

MINIATURE EDITION, 13 vols. (1870–7).

IMPERIAL LIBRARY EDITION, 6 vols. (1872–3); 7 vols. (1877).

CABINET EDITION, 13 vols. (1874–81).

AUTHOR'S EDITION, 7 vols. (1874–81).

CROWN EDITION (1878).

MACMILLANS' EDITION (1884)
—repeatedly reprinted.

EDITION-DE-LUXE, 12 vols. (1898–9)
—vols. I–IV contain a Memoir by H. Tennyson.

EVERSLEY EDITION, ed. H. Tennyson, 9 vols. (1907–8), 1 vol. (1913)

POEMS, ed. M. Bozman (1949)
—reissued, 1965.

POEMS AND PLAYS (1953).

Selected Works:

LYRICAL POEMS, ed. F. T. Palgrave (1885).

LYRICS AND POEMS, ed. E. A. Sharp, 2 vols. (1899).

THE EARLY POEMS, ed. J. C. Collins (1900).

IN MEMORIAM, THE PRINCESS, AND MAUD, ed. J. C. Collins (1902).

POEMS, ed. H. Van Dyke (1903).

POEMS, ed. H. J. C. Grierson (1907).

SHORTER POEMS AND LYRICS, 1833–42, ed. B. C. Mulliner. Oxford (1909).

SUPPRESSED POEMS, 1830–68, ed. J. C. Thompson (1910).

SELECTED POEMS, ed. C. B. Wheeler and F. A. Cavenagh. Oxford (1916).

UNPUBLISHED EARLY POEMS, ed. C. B. L. Tennyson (1931).

TENNYSON, AN ANTHOLOGY, ed. F. L. Lucas. Cambridge (1932).

SELECTED POEMS, ed. Sir J. Squire (1947).

POETRY AND PROSE, ed. F. L. Lucas. Oxford (1947).

SELECTED POEMS, ed. S. Gwynn (1950)
—supersedes the earlier World's Classics editions of 1910 and 1912.

POEMS, ed. Sir C. Tennyson (1954).

Separate Works:

POEMS, BY TWO BROTHERS (1827)
—by Alfred and Charles, with 3 or 4 pieces by Frederick.

TIMBUCTOO. Cambridge (1829)
—the rare *Prolusiones Academicae* of the year of the poem, awarded the Chancellor's Medal for English verse.

POEMS, CHIEFLY LYRICAL (1830).

POEMS (1833).

POEMS, 2 vols. (1842)
—Editions 5–8 (1848–53) in one vol. Edition 8 (1853) gives the final text.

THE PRINCESS (1847)
—Editions 3 (1850), 4 (1851), and 5 (1853) are textually important and
contain substantial revisions. Edition 5 gives the final text.

IN MEMORIAM (1850).

ODE ON THE DEATH OF THE DUKE OF WELLINGTON (1852).

MAUD, AND OTHER POEMS (1855)
—edition 3 (1856) adds 10 pages to the title-poem.

POEMS (1858)
—with illustrations by Millais, Rossetti, Holman Hunt, etc.

IDYLLS OF THE KING (1859). 'Enid', 'Vivien', 'Elaine', 'Guinevere'
—enlarged editions 1869, 1889.

ODE FOR THE OPENING OF THE INTERNATIONAL EXHIBITION (1862).

ENOCH ARDEN, ETC. (1864).

THE HOLY GRAIL AND OTHER POEMS (1870).

GARETH AND LYNETTE (1872).

QUEEN MARY (1875). *Play*

HAROLD (1877). *Play*

BECKET (1879). *Play*

THE LOVER'S TALE (1879)
—the first authorized edition.

BALLADS AND OTHER POEMS (1880).

THE CUP AND THE FALCON (1884). *Plays*

TIRESIAS AND OTHER POEMS (1885).

LOCKSLEY HALL SIXTY YEARS AFTER, ETC. (1886).

DEMETER, AND OTHER POEMS (1889).

THE FORESTERS: ROBIN HOOD AND MAID MARIAN (1892). *Play*

THE DEATH OF OENONE, AKBAR'S DREAM, AND OTHER POEMS (1892).

THE DEVIL AND THE LADY, ed. Sir C. Tennyson (1930).

Some Biographical and Critical Studies:

[J. WILSON] ('Christopher North') in *Blackwood's Magazine*, 1832
—review of *Poems*, 1830; reprinted in *Essays Critical and Imaginative*,
vol. II, 1866.

[J. W. Croker], in *Quarterly Review*, 1833.

[J. S. Mill], in *London and Westminster Review*, 1835, and *Westminster. Review*, 1843.
—the latter article reprinted in *Famous Reviews*, ed. R. B. Johnson, 1914.

TENNYSONIANA, by R. H. Shepherd (1866)
—revised and enlarged, 1879.

STUDIES IN LITERATURE, 1789–1877, by E. Dowden (1878)
—contains an essay entitled 'Mr Tennyson and Mr Browning'.

LITERARY STUDIES, by W. Bagehot, vol. II (1879).

MISCELLANIES, by A. C. Swinburne (1886).

LITERARY ESSAYS, by R. H. Hutton (1888).

ESSAYS TOWARDS A CRITICAL METHOD, by J. M. Robertson (1889).

'Tennyson as Prophet', by F. W. H. Myers. *The Nineteenth Century*, 1889.

VIEWS AND REVIEWS, by W. E. Henley (1890).

ILLUSTRATIONS OF TENNYSON, by J. C. Collins (1891).

RECORDS OF TENNYSON, RUSKIN AND THE BROWNINGS, by A. I. Ritchie (1892).

ESSAYS ON IDYLLS OF THE KIND, by H. Littledale (1893).

TENNYSON, by S. A. Brooke (1894).

HANDBOOK TO TENNYSON'S WORKS, by M. Luce (1895).

LITERARY ANECDOTES OF THE NINETEENTH CENTURY, by W. R. Nicoll and T. J. Wise, 2 vols. (1895–6).

CORRECTED IMPRESSIONS, by G. Saintsbury (1895).

A PRIMER OF TENNYSON, by W. M. Dixon (1896).

ALFRED, LORD TENNYSON, by Hallam, Lord Tennyson, 2 vols. (1897).

STUDIES OF A BIOGRAPHER, by L. Stephen, vol. II (1898).

TENNYSON, RUSKIN, MILL, AND OTHER LITERARY ESTIMATES, by F. Harrison (1899).

TENNYSON, by S. L. Gwynn (1899).

MEMORIES OF THE TENNYSONS, by H. D. Rawnsley. Glasgow (1900).

COMMENTARY ON IN MEMORIAM, by A. C. Bradley (1901).

TENNYSON, by A. Lang (1901).

TENNYSON, by A. Lyall (1902).

'Personal Recollections of Tennyson', by W. G. MacCabe, *The Century Illustrated Monthly Magazine*, 1902.

TENNYSON, by G. K. Chesterton and R. Garnett (1903).

TENNYSON, by A. C. Benson (1904).

MODERN STUDIES, by O. Elton (1907).

TENNYSON AND HIS FRIENDS, by Hallam, Lord Tennyson (1911).

A HISTORY OF ENGLISH PROSODY, by G. Saintsbury (1906–10).

CONCORDANCE TO THE POETICAL AND DRAMATICAL WORKS, by A. E. Baker (1914)
—Supplement, 1931.

LIFE AND TIMES OF TENNYSON FROM 1809 TO 1850, by T. R. Loundsbury, ed. W. L. Cross. New Haven (1915).

A TENNYSON DICTIONARY, by A. E. Baker (1916).

A SURVEY OF ENGLISH LITERATURE, 1830–80, by O. Elton, vol. I (1920).

'The Idylls of the King in 1921', by F. S. Boas, *Transactions of Royal Society of Literature*, 1922.

TENNYSON, by H. I'A. Faussett (1923).

TENNYSON, by H. Nicolson (1923).

COLLECTED ESSAYS, by W. P. Ker, vol. I (1925).

'Personal Recollections of Tennyson', by W. F. Rawnsley, *The Nineteenth Century*, 1925

STUDIES OF ENGLISH POETS, by J. W. Mackail (1926).

SELECTED ESSAYS, by E. Gosse, vol. I (1928).

A MISCELLANY, by A. C. Bradley (1929).

EIGHT VICTORIAN POETS, by F. L. Lucas (1930)
—republished 1940, as *Ten Victorian Poets*.

TENNYSON, by H. Wolfe (1930).

REVALUATIONS, by L. Abercrombie (1931).

'Tennyson's Unpublished Poems', by Sir C. Tennyson, *The Nineteenth Century*, 1931.

TENNYSON, by A. Noyes. Edinburgh (1932).

THE POET AS CITIZEN, by A. T. Quiller Couch (1934).

'Tennyson Papers', by Sir C. Tennyson, *Cornhill Magazine*, 1936.

ESSAYS ANCIENT AND MODERN, T. S. Eliot (1936).

THE TIME OF TENNYSON, by C. Weygandt. New York (1936).

'The Age of Tennyson', by G. M. Young, *Proceedings of the British Academy*, 1939.

TENNYSON SIXTY YEARS AFTER, by P. F. Baum. Chapel Hill, N. Carolina (1948).

TENNYSON, by Sir C. Tennyson (1949).

'Wordsworth and Tennyson', by D. G. James, *Proceedings of the British Academy*, 1950.

TENNYSON AND THE REVIEWERS, by E. F. Shannon. Cambridge, Mass. (1952).

THE ALIEN VISION OF VICTORIAN POETRY, by E. D. H. Johnson. Princeton (1952).

SIX TENNYSON ESSAYS, by Sir C. Tennyson (1954).

TENNYSON AND THE PRINCESS, by J. Killham (1958).

CRITICAL ESSAYS ON THE POETRY OF TENNYSON, J. Killham (1960).

TENNYSON, by J. H. Buckley. Cambridge, Mass. (1960).

TENNYSON, LAUREATE, by V. J. Pitt (1962).

THE PRE-EMINENT VICTORIAN, by J. Richardson (1962).

CATALOGUE OF AN EXHIBITION AT THE USHER GALLERY, LINCOLN. Lincoln (1963)
—contains a foreword by Sir C. Tennyson.

TENNYSON'S MAUD, by R. W. Rader. Los Angeles (1963).

THEME AND SYMBOL IN TENNYSON'S POEMS to 1850, by C. de L. Ryals. Philadelphia (1964).